DRAW MANGA

Peter Gray

ARCTURUS

Arcturus Publishing Limited
26/27 Bickels Yard
151–153 Bermondsey Street
London SE1 3HA

Published in association with
foulsham
W. Foulsham & Co. Ltd,
The Publishing House, Bennetts Close, Cippenham,
Slough, Berkshire SL1 5AP, England

ISBN 0-572-03013-4

British Library Cataloguing-in-Publication Data: a catalogue record for this
book is available from the British Library

Artwork by Peter Gray
Cover and book design by Steve Flight
Character design based on original artwork by Ben Krefta

Printed in Singapore

CONTENTS

INTRODUCTION 4
MATERIALS 5

FACES

ARIEL 6
BLAZE 8
SERENA 10
X-O-DUS 12

EXPRESSIONS

ARIEL 14
BLAZE 15
SERENA 16
X-O-DUS 17

FIGURES

ARIEL 18
BLAZE 20
SERENA 22
X-O-DUS 24

ACTION

ARIEL 26
BLAZE 27
SERENA 28
X-O-DUS 29

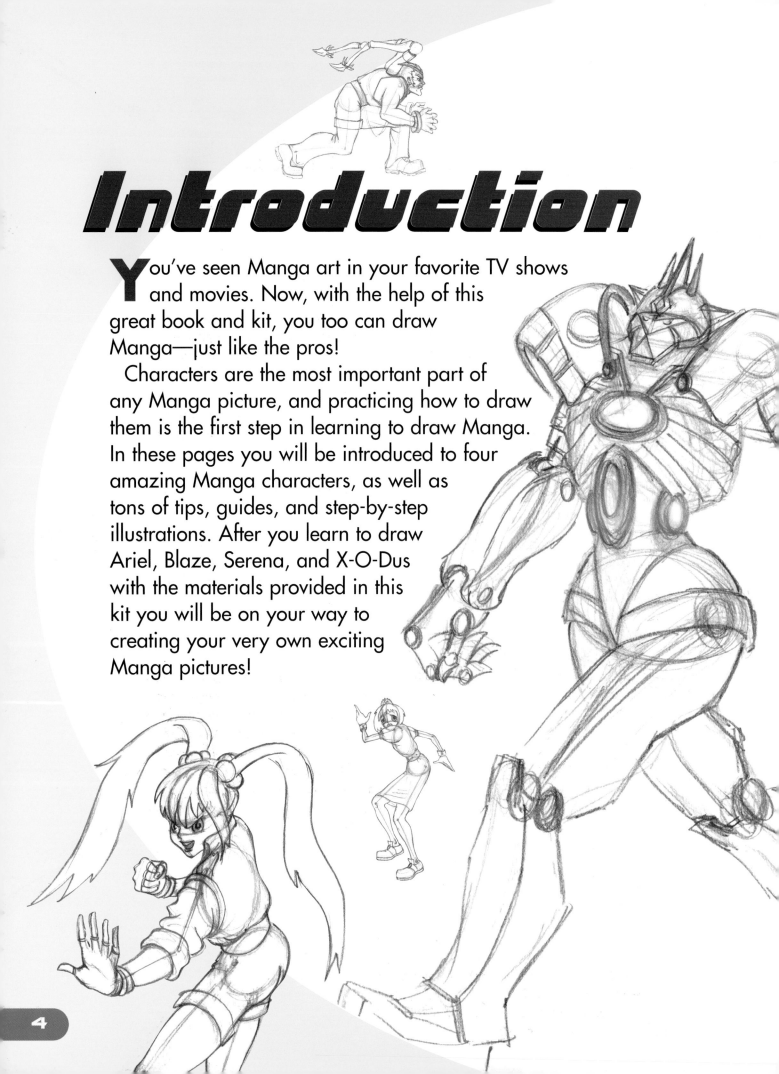

Introduction

You've seen Manga art in your favorite TV shows and movies. Now, with the help of this great book and kit, you too can draw Manga—just like the pros!

Characters are the most important part of any Manga picture, and practicing how to draw them is the first step in learning to draw Manga. In these pages you will be introduced to four amazing Manga characters, as well as tons of tips, guides, and step-by-step illustrations. After you learn to draw Ariel, Blaze, Serena, and X-O-Dus with the materials provided in this kit you will be on your way to creating your very own exciting Manga pictures!

Materials

Everything you need to get started:

Paper

Good-quality drawing paper is ideal for your Manga creations, but if you can't stretch to it, use an artist's sketchbook instead.

Mechanical pencils with refills

These hard pencils are great because they make thin, clean lines—and they never need sharpening.

Soft graphite pencils

Soft pencils make thick, heavy lines. They are great for tones and shading, but can be messy because they smudge easily. B is a medium-weight pencil; 2B is heavier.

Coloured pencils

These come in a range of colours. Remember, always make your characters brighter than the background so that they stand out.

Pencil sharpener

A sharp pencil is very important.

Eraser

At first you'll be using it to correct mistakes, but as you get more skilled you'll also use the eraser to create special effects and to clean up your final drawings.

Ruler

Don't be afraid to use a ruler—not everyone can draw a straight line freehand without a lot of practice.

Rectangular stencils

These will help you draw the shapes that make up each character's figure.

Black paint

This paint is good for outlining your final drawing.

White paint

This paint can be used to correct mistakes or even add special effects, like beams of light.

Paint brushes

Try to equip yourself with paintbrushes of varying thicknesses. To begin, one thin brush and one thick one should be adequate for your needs. Many artists use brushes, but they do take getting used to, and you will have to develop a feel for them. Practice painting over your pencil outlines to develop this and boost your confidence.

WARNING: Be sure to prepare your work space properly, covering it with newspaper or some other disposable material before you begin. Remember, the paint can stain!

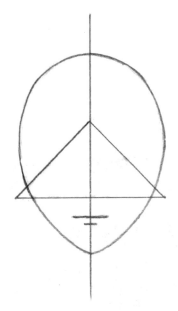

Stage 1 ▶

Although it might seem a little boring, it is very important in drawing to get the foundations right before you add detail. Draw the basic upside-down egg shape, making it quite broad and pointed at the bottom.
For Ariel's eyes, draw a shallow triangle across your egg shape.

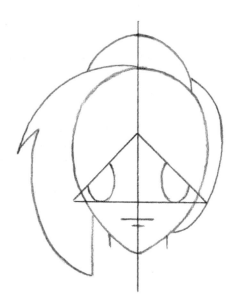

◀ Stage 2

Treat Ariel's hair as a series of basic shapes before going on to more detail later. Just draw some curves at this stage. If you draw these curves quickly, they will be smoother. Put in the rough shape of Ariel's headband on top of her head. Working within your triangle, sketch in some big round eyes. Where the triangle crosses your center line, that's where the nose goes.

Stage 3 ▶

Build up the detail in the hair, keeping the lines flowing and graceful. Add more detail around the eyes with gentle S-shaped eyelids and also sketch in her eyebrows.

◀ Stage 4

By this stage all the hard work is done and you only need to clean up your drawing and add a few details to the eyes and headband. Remember to erase all your rough guidelines. Ariel's nose is hardly more than a dot from this angle. Try to capture her slightly sad little smile.

Profile

Name: **Ariel**

Age: **16**

Skill: **Magic**

On the surface, Ariel is a happy and care-free girl, just like her other friends in the village. Fond of entertaining, she can often be seen singing and dancing in the town hall. But Ariel had always sensed that she was different, that she didn't quite belong, and now she's learned the truth: She is half human, half sprite—and she has the power of magic. Now she must seek out the true nature of her gift, and her destiny. . . .

◄ 3/4 View ►

It's really good practice to shade things in pencil. As you get better at it, you will see how effective basic pencils can be in bringing your pictures to life. A good tip is to use the full range of tone from the white of the paper down to the darkest marks that your pencils can make.

◄ Profile ►

Ariel is a simple soul, and this is echoed in her design. Simple curves make up her face from every angle. Be gentle with your colored pencils—you may need to use only light pressure with your orange and pink pencils to capture her skin tones. Make her hair very dark and rich as a contrast. Here I've pressed very hard with the blue pencil and darkened it in the shadow areas with a 2B pencil.

Faces

Stage 1 ▶

Blaze is much more rugged than Ariel, and his proportions are closer to those of a real person. Draw a circle for his skull and then add lines for his strong jaw. The eye lines come just under halfway down the head. The bottom line of the nose rests along the bottom of your circle and the mouth line just a short distance under that.

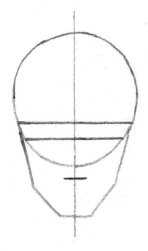

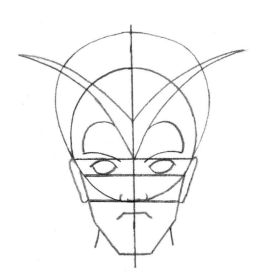

◀ Stage 2

Add a bigger arch around the top for Blaze's hair, which is one of his strongest features. Put in guidelines for his forehead and antennae. Pay close attention to the shape of his eyes and eyebrows. Don't forget Blaze's ears. They join his head along the same lines as his eyes and the bottom of his nose.

Stage 3 ▶

As his name suggests, Blaze's hair looks a bit like flames sweeping up from his brow and back over his head. Try to get that feel as you put in his spikes. Remember his sideburns, even though you can't see much of them from this angle. Start to add details to his eyes, nose, and mouth.

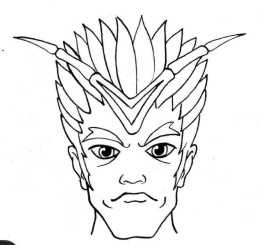

◀ Stage 4

Use darker pencils to finish Blaze's features. Make the jawline really rugged and get the right expression in his down-turned mouth. Blaze's face has a lot of character, and drawing in the frown lines around his eyes will make all the difference in the mood of your drawing.

Name: **Blaze**

Age: **17**

Skill: **Super strength**

Blaze was just an ordinary boy when he was taken from his parents during the Star Conflict and captured by the Kiras, a destructive race of cybernetic spiders. The Kiras, who used Blaze for a number of gruesome genetic experiments—including one that left him with biomechanical arms—didn't take into account their prey's incredible thirst for survival. Refusing to buckle under torture, Blaze turned the Kiras' own weapons against them, using his new arms to escape the enemy stronghold.

Ruthless and single-minded, Blaze has built a fearsome reputation among his allies and enemies alike, particularly among the Kiras, who he has vowed he will destroy if it's the last thing he ever does. . . .

◄ 3/4 View ►

When you draw characters from different angles, your guidelines are important. It doesn't matter if you don't get them right the first time—they will all be erased in the end, anyway. Use the darker pencils for shading (B, 2B). Use the B first to gently shade all the gray areas and then go over the details with your 2B. Don't forget that your eraser can be very useful for highlights as well as erasing mistakes.

◄ Profile ►

Working out the profile is a good way of getting to know your character. Blaze looks even grumpier from the side, but his proportions are the same as from the front. If you're working with colored pencils, remember that you can blend the colors together and even use graphite pencils on top or underneath them. Tone down the yellow of Blaze's hair if you can.

Stage 1 ▶

Start with faint guidelines using a light pencil (the 0.7 or 0.5 mechanical pencil) that you can erase later. Use a basic oval, like an egg with the pointed end down, and draw a straight line down the center. Just below halfway draw a horizontal line for the top of Serena's eyes and another a little lower for the bottom of her eyes. A gentle curve that meets the top eyeline will guide you for drawing her bangs and eyebrows.

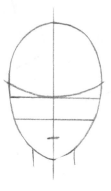

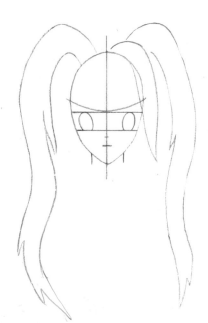

◀ Stage 2

Keep building up the basic shapes with your light pencil. Add in flowing lines for Serena's hair and sketch in her big oval eyes, following the guidelines you have already drawn. Remember to have fun. You don't have to copy everything exactly. Why not play around with Serena's hair shape?

Stage 3 ▶

Work on some of the details, following your guidelines. Draw in the eyebrows and eyelashes and give her some large oval pupils. The face needs to be shaped into cheeks and a slightly pointed chin. Build up the spiky shapes of her hair. Also work on drawing the texture of her hair.

◀ Stage 4

As you get closer to the final face, start going over your good lines with a darker pencil (B) and erase your guidelines. Serena's eyes are very important to her character, so pay close attention to them with your darkest pencil (B). Use the corner of your eraser to lift out some highlights in her eyes. If you want to, you can use your black paint for this final stage of drawing. Make sure that it is dry before you erase all your rough lines.

Serena

Profile

Name: **Serena**

Age: **15**

Skill: **Jujitsu**

Serena is certainly a *Bishoujo*, a beautiful girl—but she is not just a pretty face. When her younger brother was disfigured in a running battle with a rival school Serena took it upon herself to seek revenge. Vowing to find those responsible, she ended up in a show-down with the ringleader of the notorious Blood Gang, and she avenged her brother, using a combination of jujitsu and street smarts. Now, her fate as a righter of wrongs revealed to her, Serena's fierce quest for justice continues. . . .

◄ 3/4 View ►

This is a more complicated angle to draw Serena from. See how the central line curves? It is important to use guidelines for drawings like this so that you can place the features correctly. Get the basic shapes right from the start and your drawing should fall into place. The finished picture was completed using the graphite pencils in your kit. Graphite pencils are beginner friendly —you can erase mistakes very easily!

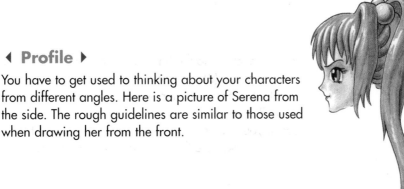

◄ Profile ►

You have to get used to thinking about your characters from different angles. Here is a picture of Serena from the side. The rough guidelines are similar to those used when drawing her from the front.

Faces

Stage 1 ▶

Because it is a mecha, X-O-Dus is the most demanding character to draw in this book, so make good use of your ruler and mechanical pencil. Begin with a long vertical line, then draw a smooth arch across the top. Copy the arched shapes that make up its jawline and the horizontal line for its chin. Now you must build up a kind of grid to fit its features onto. Draw a horizontal and then two vertical lines going up from the corners of the chin. Join up those lines with curves that follow the lines of the jaw.

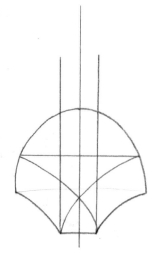

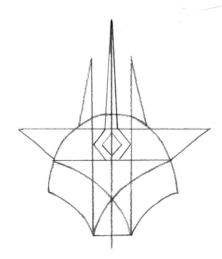

◀ Stage 2

Now we can add some spikes and build up more guidelines as we go. Use the ruler to draw another horizontal line just below the crown of the helmet. Join the ends of that line to the side of the helmet at the points where your curved lines end. On either side of your two outer vertical lines, draw the other edges of the "horn" spikes and then form the middle vertical into another spike for its antennae. You should now have a neat rectangle in the middle of the brow. Fill in a neat hexagon and a diamond shape within that.

Stage 3 ▶

The next pieces of drawing are quite simple but will make all the difference in the finished picture. Break up the curve of the jaw and chin area. When you add the extra lines inside your new jawline, you will see that this makes the picture look more 3-D. A couple more straight lines inside the "ear" spikes will have the same effect there too.

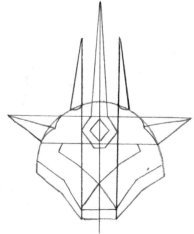

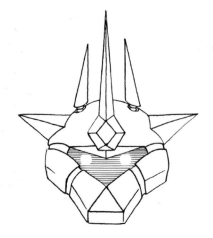

◀ Stage 4

The head is a combination of straight lines and curves, so look carefully at the picture in the book and try to get the lines right. Inside the visor, X-O-Dus has shutters that it can close for protection. Here the shutters are only slightly closed. Shade in the rest of the visor with a dark pencil and pick out some highlights with your eraser for the powerful beams of its eyes.

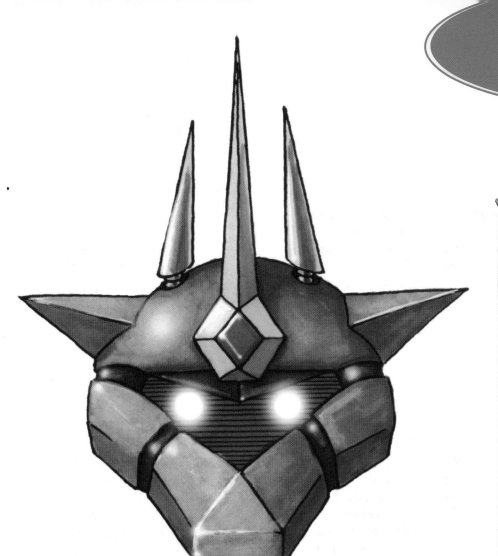

Profile

Name: **X-O-Dus**

Description: **52 feet; 9.5 tons; made of titanium alloy**

Weapons: **Missiles; heat deflectors; head Vulcans**

The mecha X-O-Dus is heavily armored and equipped for close combat fighting. It is piloted by a mysterious mercenary known only as Quarg. Its main weapons are missiles, and it also has heat deflectors and head vulcans for long-range support. It looks like a very simple mecha—but it should not be underestimated!

X-O-Dus was last seen wreaking havoc in the Third Mecha Wars when Quarg single-handedly stormed and destroyed the Imperial Palace for the Free Army. . . .

◀ 3/4 View ▶

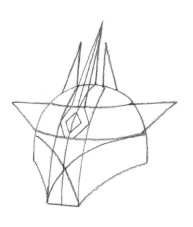

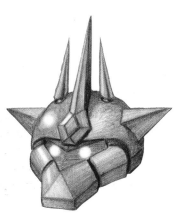

Following similar guidelines to our first drawing of X-O-Dus makes its helmet seem to bow outward. As you work up the drawing, you will change the lines as you go through the stages, but you need them to show how the parts of its head join together. When shading in, bear in mind that it has a kind of dull metallic surface with deep shadows and bright highlights. You might find your eraser very useful as you finish the drawing.

◀ Profile ▶

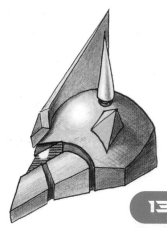

Looking at X-O-Dus's helmet from the side shows us how things can look very different depending on your viewpoint. The construction lines that we used in drawing it from the front are not really visible here, so pay attention to getting the curves just right. The basic head shape is like half a ball, so when you are ready to color or shade this shape, why not find a ball at home and see how the light falls on it and how the shadow gives it roundness? X-O-Dus is also good shading and coloring practice because its helmet is made up of flat and curved surfaces, all of which reflect the light differently.

Ariel wears her heart on her sleeve. Like Serena, her hair can be used to echo how she feels, as can her large eyes and expressive mouth. When you are working on expressions, don't be afraid to make mistakes. It does take practice to get them right. You can get some scrap paper and fill it with dozens of little sketches of your characters feeling every different kind of emotion that you can think of. Make these sketches quick and simple, and don't worry too much about detail. Pick out the ones that work best to copy onto good paper for finished drawings.

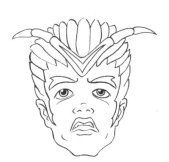

Blaze is a tough guy and doesn't usually display a great deal of emotion in his face, but it is still important for the artist to know how he will look in different situations. He is human and will sometimes show degrees of happiness or fear along with his more usual stern expression. A lot of artists use mirrors to help them get facial expressions right. Try it yourself: Sit in front of a mirror when you are drawing and look at your own face as you make the expression you are trying to draw. Although your own face will look different from your characters', it will help you to see how to change their features for different moods.

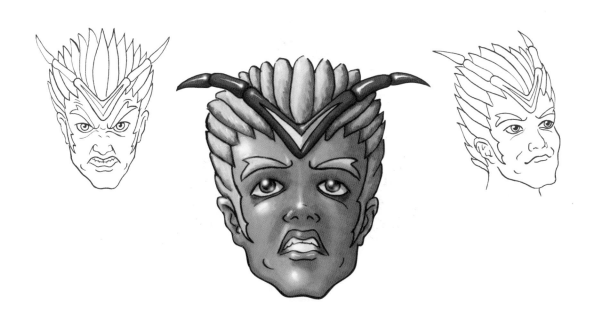

Serena is essentially a fighter who likes to have fun, and often this shows in her face. She also has another side to her character, which can be more gentle. When you draw or invent characters, try to think about all the different moods they might show at different times. Faces can be very expressive, and it's important to show how characters are feeling or what kind of personality they have. To show different moods, you can use more than just their facial features. For example, when Serena is sad, her hair becomes less bouncy and her face is downcast. The position or angle of the head can often say a great deal about a character.

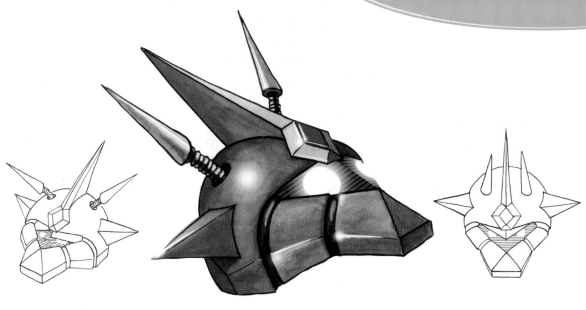

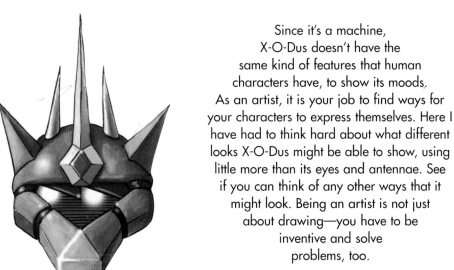

Since it's a machine, X-O-Dus doesn't have the same kind of features that human characters have, to show its moods. As an artist, it is your job to find ways for your characters to express themselves. Here I have had to think hard about what different looks X-O-Dus might be able to show, using little more than its eyes and antennae. See if you can think of any other ways that it might look. Being an artist is not just about drawing—you have to be inventive and solve problems, too.

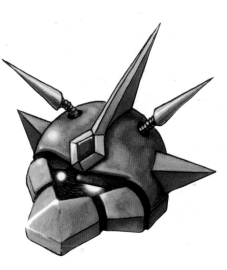

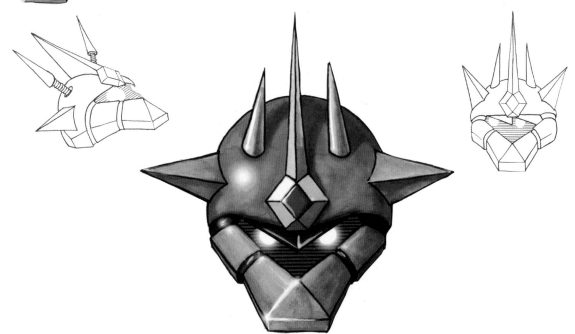

Figures

Stage 1

Even when drawing a character in a simple standing pose, you can say a lot about her with her body language. Ariel is quite innocent and girlish, and this is shown in the way she stands, which is very different from the aggressive stance of the other characters. This kind of feeling should be clear from the earliest stage of your drawings.

Stage 2

Ariel is very slim, but even the skinniest bodies have curves. When you draw her body, pay attention to the shapes of her shoulders and legs in particular.

Stage 3

All the elements of drawing a character should say something about their personality. This neat, fitted dress says a lot about what kind of person Ariel is and how she is different from the fighting characters. Hands can say a lot about a person too, so be careful to capture Ariel's long, delicate fingers.

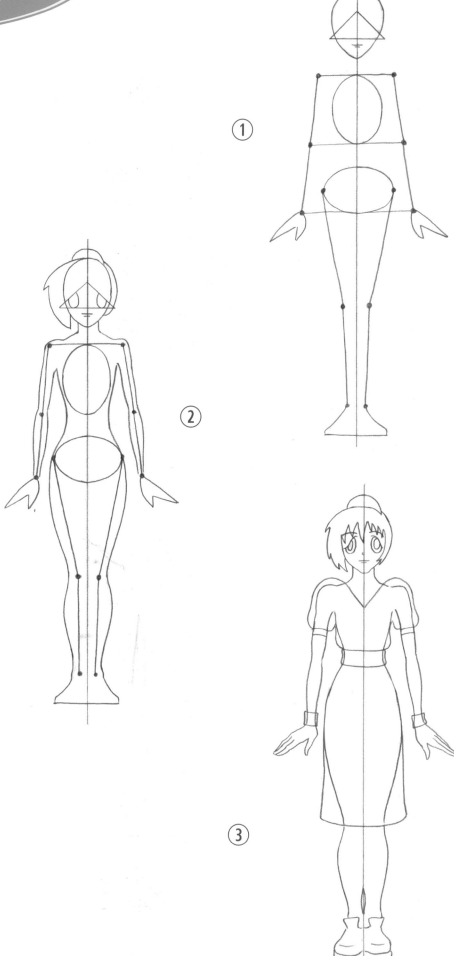

④

⑤

Stage 4

There's not a lot left to do to finish this picture. A few pieces of jewelry and some cleaning up, and you will have the picture complete in no time. You can add extra details of your own if you like. It's your drawing, so don't feel you have to stick with what you see here.

Stage 5

Ariel's colors are bright and simple, but to make the clothing look realistic, it's a good idea to mix some blue in with the purple for the shadows. You could give her dress a pattern or design, or even change the colors completely. Remember, making pictures should be fun!

Stage 1

Start with Blaze's skeleton. His construction is pretty much the same as Ariel's, but the proportions are very different. His chest and shoulders are very broad and his stance is wider. Keep those legs nice and long. Many Manga characters have very long legs.

Stage 2

Drawing Blaze's body shape is quite complicated because he has such big muscles. It might help you if you notice that he is narrower at the joints, elbows, knees, and wrists. The more you draw from copying pictures in magazines or comics, the better you will become at knowing the shapes of muscles.

Stage 3

Blaze's clothes are quite easy to draw once you have his body shape drawn because they follow the shapes quite closely. Add some flesh to his extra arms and work on those hands and shoes.

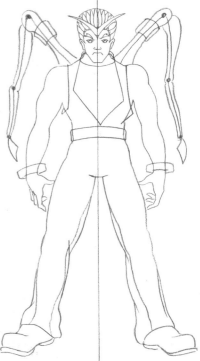

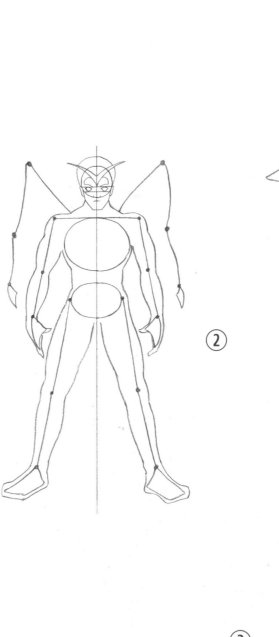

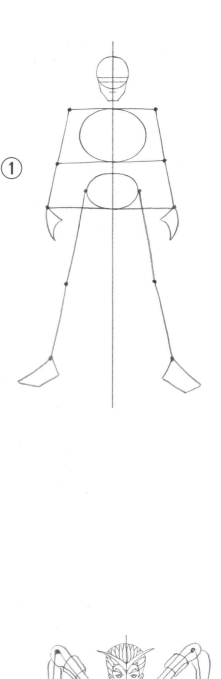

④

⑤

Stage 4

A few extra details, some wrinkles on the pants, and a bit of cleaning up should give you a finished-looking drawing. You can add tattoos down his arms and some texture to his extra arms if you like, and then you should be ready to color.

Stage 5

Because he is a dark and mysterious character, you should show this with heavy colors and lots of black and dark gray. A touch of purple around the eyes will give him a mean and scary look.

Figures

Stage 1

Serena's skeleton shows her proportions as well as where all her joints are. Draw ovals for her chest and hips, and these will help you to draw the width of her body. Leave space under her head for a neck, and draw in those broad shoulders and long legs. You might want to use your ruler to measure the right lengths for your drawing.

Stage 2

Draw in the outline of Serena's body. If you have gotten the skeleton right, the body should be easy to work out. Don't worry about hands and feet at this point but do sketch in a rough shape so that you know what size to draw them at the next stage.

Stage 3

When you're happy with Serena's body shape, start sketching in her clothes around it. You might like to erase the skeleton as you go. If you drew this lightly, it should erase easily. As you get closer to the finished drawing, you could use darker pencils. Pay attention to where the clothing wrinkles around her arms and waist and start working on her hands too.

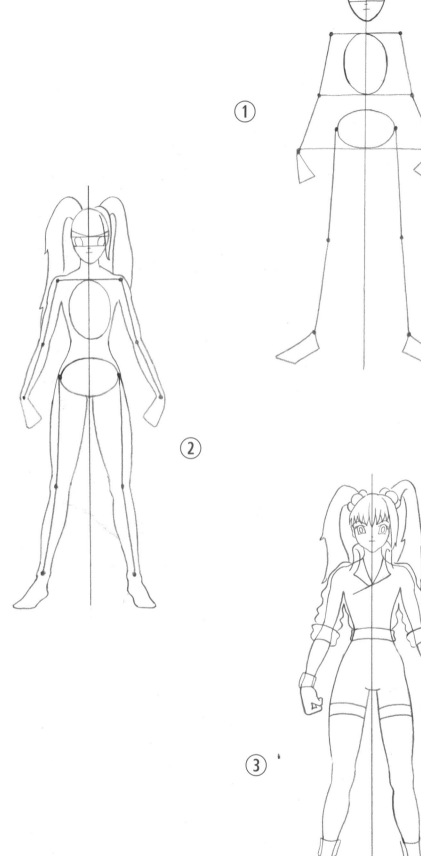

Serena

④

⑤

Stage 4

All those little features like her belt buckle and gloves add a lot of character to your drawing. It's also worth spending some time to get the hands and shoes drawn well. They are often the test of a good drawing.

Stage 5

The main feature of coloring Serena is the leathery surface of her clothes. It's probably best if you use your graphite pencils for the black leather and leave some highlights to give it a shiny appearance.

Figures

Stage 1

This is by far the most difficult character to draw, so be prepared to spend some time getting each stage just right before you add too much detail. Because it is a mecha, X-O-Dus has a very different kind of skeleton. It is still basically human in shape but broader and with big joints, some of which will show in the final drawing. You're only blocking in rough shapes at the moment, but try to get the proportions right.

Stage 2

The body shape here is more like armor than flesh. Shoulders, hips, and limbs are all huge except for its upper arms, which have no armor because they are protected by the shoulder armor and need to be able to move freely.

Stage 3

You have to think three-dimensionally and try to show in a few simple lines the solidity of this powerful robot. Just like its helmet, X-O-Dus's body is a mixture of curves and angles. It might help you to erase some of your guidelines as you go at this stage so that you don't get confused.

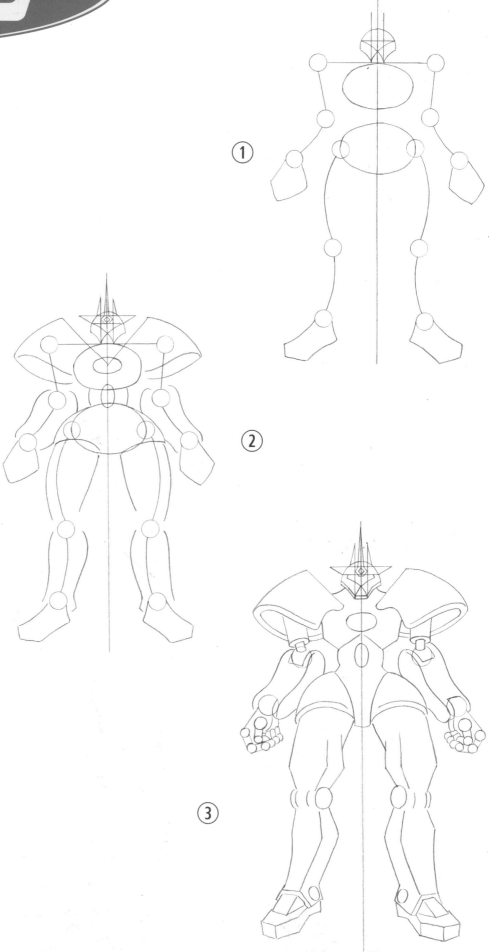

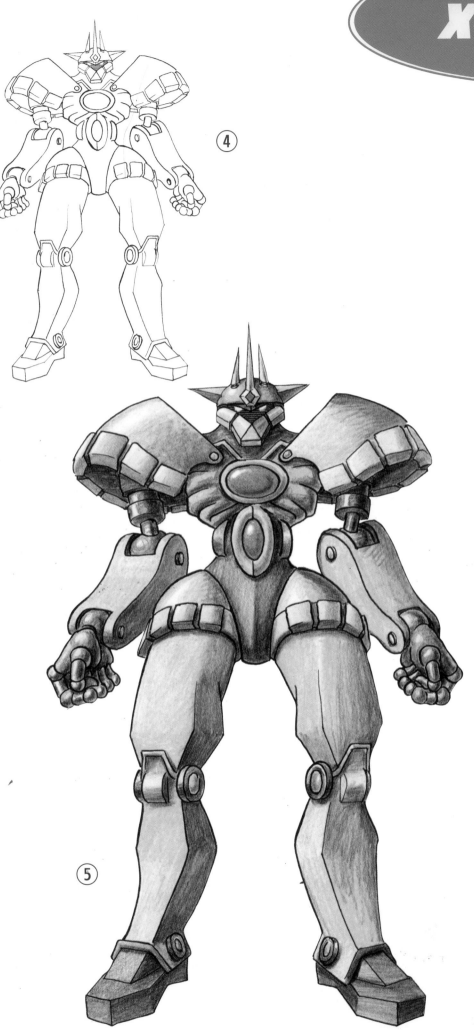

④

⑤

Stage 4

Adding the details to X-O-Dus will give it that hard, military look. Make your final drawing really solid and you should have a mean fighting machine who will strike fear into the heart of its enemies. Don't forget to draw its joints. That will imply the way it moves in battle and add to its scariness.

Stage 5

You don't need to be so smooth when coloring X-O-Dus. Get across the fact that it is made of metal, which shines in places, and is duller where it is painted green. Leaving the paper white in places can be very effective, so be careful with those colored pencils. They are not as easy to erase as your graphite pencils. You can use your white paint to add highlights at the end.

Action

Stage 1

Try a delicate pose for Ariel. Her left arm is slightly foreshortened, and we are taking a low viewpoint. Also, her left leg looks as if it is bending back. Artists often exaggerate details like this; here it will help to show that her weight is supported by that leg.

Stage 2

The curved center lines you drew on Ariel's skeleton will help you to understand the direction her body is facing.

Stage 3

Adding Ariel's clothes is quite straightforward, but look out for her left sleeve, which is hidden behind her hand. The curve of her wristband helps to show the angles of her arms and hide her delicate wrists. Make sure that you keep her fingers long and slender.

Stage 4

Just a few jewels to add at this stage. It's sometimes fun to play around with characters, and with Ariel there is a nice contrast between her feminine manner and clothing and those big chunky shoes. Decorating them with the same jewels makes the whole outfit work together.

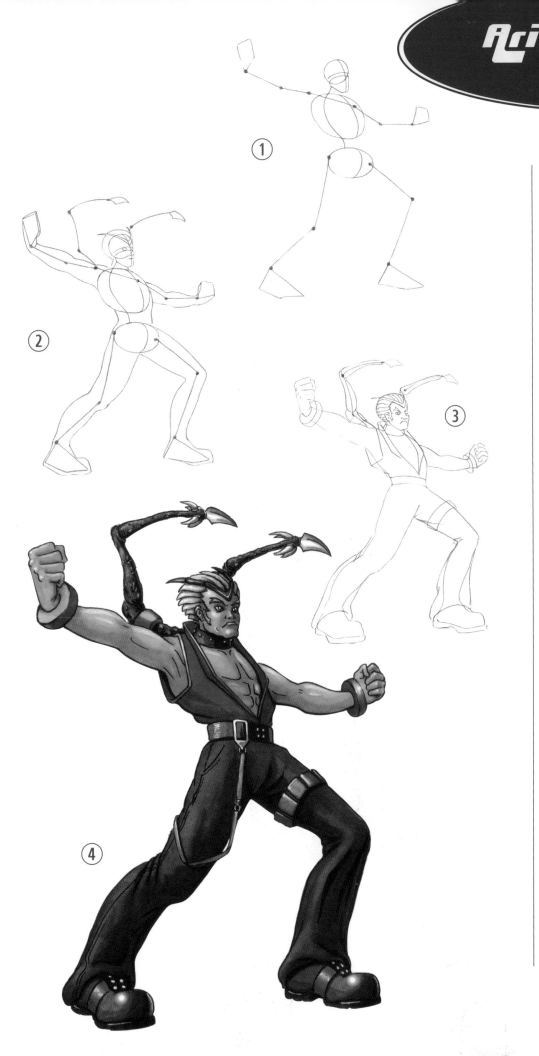

Stage 1

In this picture of Blaze we will consider another skill—a low viewpoint. Imagine that you are sitting on the floor and looking up at Blaze standing in front of you. Because you are lower than he is, the right arm will appear to be higher than the left. You might also notice that his left shoulder is hidden behind his chest.

Stage 2

This is the tricky part. The skeleton will help you a lot, but you also have to think about the muscles. Pay attention to the knees, wrists, and especially the ankles since we want to make him appear to be standing solidly on the ground.

Stage 3

Blaze's clothing should be quite easy for you to draw in now, along with his extra arms. See how big his feet look compared to his head. This is because of the low viewpoint, which means they appear closer to us.

Stage 4

Again, it is the details that make the picture really come to life. The stern expression, the wrinkles of the pants, and the clenched fists are all important to show a character who is ready for action.

Action

Stage 1

Start with the basic skeleton. Notice that the center lines curve around her head, chest, and pelvis to show the way the body will twist. The right forearm is very short because it will be pointing toward us. This is what artists call foreshortening.

Stage 2

Serena's body shape is not at all symmetrical because of the pose we are drawing. Draw her hair flowing behind her to convey her movement as she jumps through the air.

Stage 3

You've done the hard work; now you can enjoy putting in the details of her clothes. The jacket is wrinkled on one side of the arm and pulled tight on the other to add to the realism of the pose. Get the right expression on Serena's face here. This is a fighting pose, so her face should look determined.

Stage 4

As you finish your drawing, you might like to think about how the elements of pose, hair, clothing, and expression all work together to give the illusion of movement to Serena.

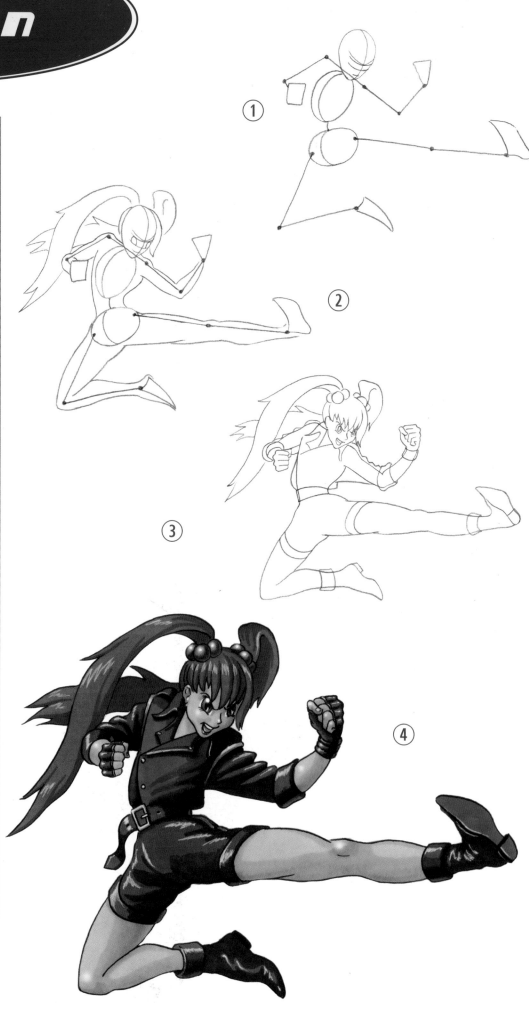

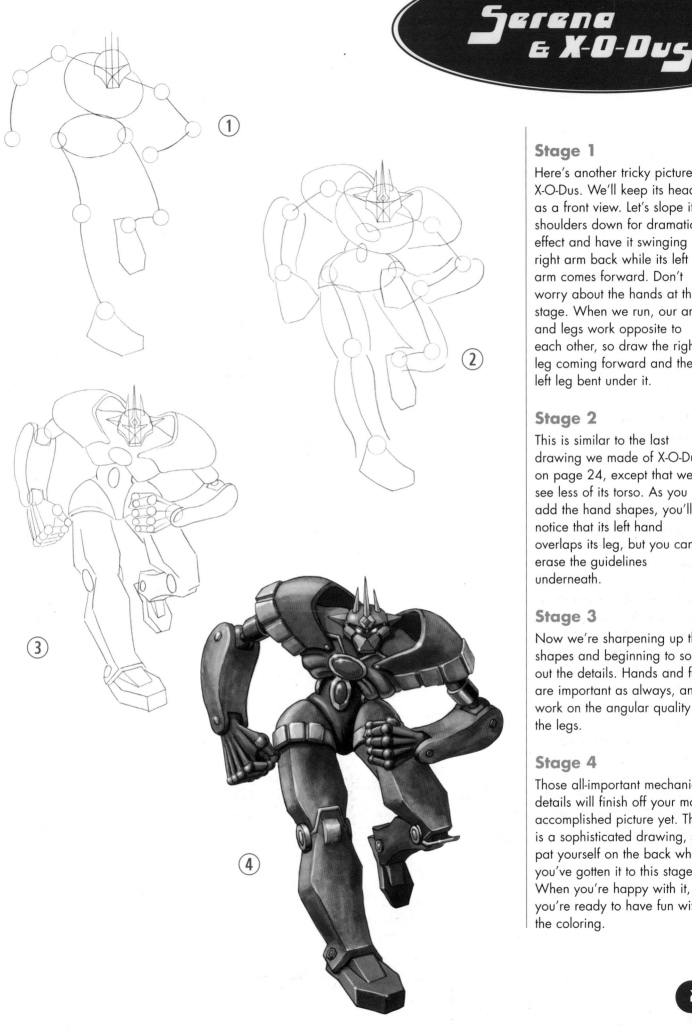

Stage 1

Here's another tricky picture of X-O-Dus. We'll keep its head as a front view. Let's slope its shoulders down for dramatic effect and have it swinging its right arm back while its left arm comes forward. Don't worry about the hands at this stage. When we run, our arms and legs work opposite to each other, so draw the right leg coming forward and the left leg bent under it.

Stage 2

This is similar to the last drawing we made of X-O-Dus on page 24, except that we'll see less of its torso. As you add the hand shapes, you'll notice that its left hand overlaps its leg, but you can erase the guidelines underneath.

Stage 3

Now we're sharpening up the shapes and beginning to sort out the details. Hands and feet are important as always, and work on the angular quality of the legs.

Stage 4

Those all-important mechanical details will finish off your most accomplished picture yet. This is a sophisticated drawing, so pat yourself on the back when you've gotten it to this stage. When you're happy with it, you're ready to have fun with the coloring.

Blaze

Serena

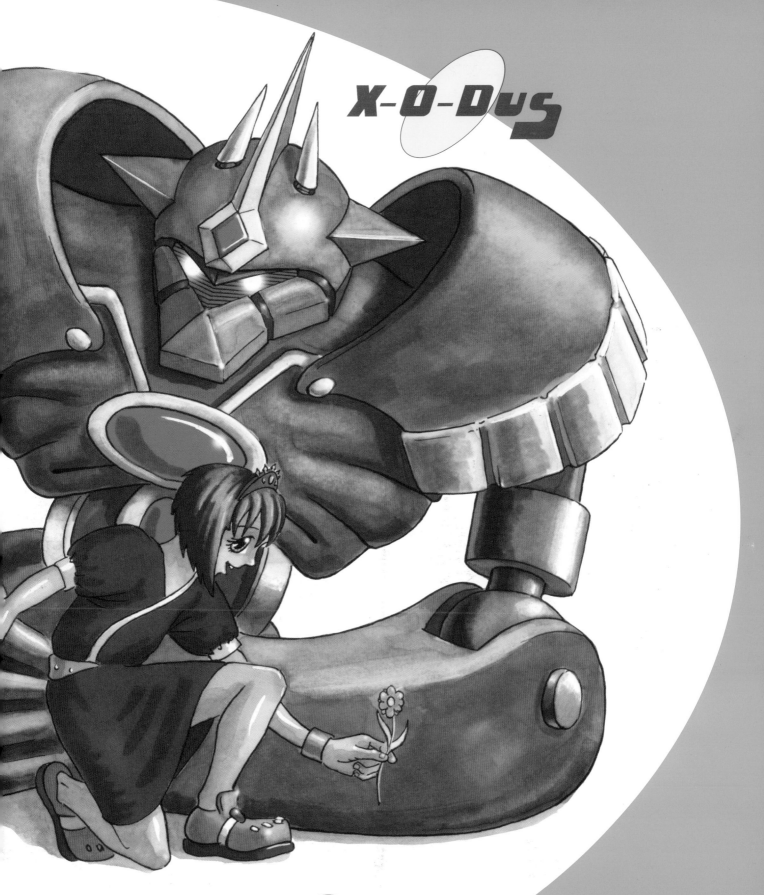

MANGA

PETER GRAY, Manga Super-fan, has always enjoyed drawing. Playing Nintendo and watching Anime cartoons made him realize that Manga was a style of art he really wanted to get into. Since Manga is so different from traditional art, Peter has lots of fun trying out different ideas, and the Manga stories themselves have opened up many possibilities for him to try out new characters.

Now he hopes that *you* will have fun creating your very own Manga artwork!